I'm that Girl Only If You Knew

Kendra D. Fullmore

Acknowledgements

In this accomplishment, many people have pushed me heard me out, always saw the best in me, even when I could not see the gifts God gave me or even potential. I want to say you all spoke nothing, but life into me, offered many blessing and whole-heartedly pledged support. I want to thank everyone in their respectable places and thank my Father the most high and wonderful God I serve God himself for imparting in me the opportunity and vision to write this novel about my very own life.

I want to give recognition to individuals who help me with brainstorming on this project my Pastor Gossypia Makinwa- Marks for giving me the word of the Lord as he commanded me to write this book and to tell the truth in the book. My brother Marcus thank you for the project and insight as to my cover illustrations and seeing the big picture. Angela Thomas-Henry for editing my book thank you for taking the time out to give up your time and help me revise the finished product. Shanika Vail-House for giving me insight on the process of publishing.

Primarily, I want to thank my wonderful parents Robin Epps-Greene (mother), Kenyatt Fullmore (father) these two continue to fuss and get onto me, but through it all they pushed me to where saw I was supposed to be in life and vision they always

Contents

longed for me. I want to thank my step parents Aundreal Fullmore for always telling what I need to hear, not what I want to hear, and believing in me, Carl Kincade for being there when no one else was, never giving up on me, believing in my visions, and helping me always. Mr. Melvin Greene for always having the most encouraging words to say. My siblings Carlas (Caree) Kincade, Caleb Kincade, Precious Fullmore, and Marcus Key you all are such an asset to me I stand as a role model and a big sister; just seeing you all's face make me want to lead and be a big sister the one I am supposed to be. My grandma Catherine Epps my every best friend and loving my dear angel God has giving to me. My grandmother Helen Wright who is always so gracious to me and anything I do. My granny Elizabeth Jones who is always my outlet and wisdom giver. My aunts for being the aunts they are and more treating me as if I am their child. All my uncles thank you for being my special protectors. My Aunt Aldyn Epps for encouraging me to DO me. My Aunt Belinda Bess who always has open arms and daughter Christi Hines, husband Chris Hines, and family who has always been a complete role model to me watched as an infant, toddlers, and in my teenager years. They have always implemented nothing but good things, cherishing me, and spoiling me. My cousins Shawn Epps-Bynes, husband Mario Bynes, and family for always let me in their home to stay, spoiling me too, and going beyond. Shay Epps for listening to me to complain, whine, pout but tell me what is best. All my other thousands of cousins and family members it is so many to list out because it is so many of you all I love you all so much and dearly. To my very best friends Breanna Tippins and Anesia Jones and my college best friends Charlotte Cropper, Shericka Bates, and Wynonna Williams, Zakiya Featherspoon who are always there to hear me, guide me, be a sister, get their best friend in trouble, but real, and true to our relationship. My god sister and brother Charity and Christian Mackey I love you zall.

All the Pastors, Prophets, and Minister who prayed for me, guided me spiritually, told me what God say even if I did not want to hear it, and every word spoken was true, and every word spoke came to pass and is still yet to manifest. Thank you, Pastors Carl Mackey and Jennifer Mann-Mackey, Pastor Gossypia Makinwa-Marks, Prophetess Alesia Guyton, Dr./Missionary Barbara Brock-Curry, all church members/congregations, and anyone else I did not list. Thank you all so much for giving me the word of the Lord obeying God, I know I was hard headed at times and did not listen. You all kept praying for me and pushing me spiritually, physically, and mentally. Thank you soooooooooooooooo much for the prayers, phone calls, and all you do, done, and continue to do it is honored and valued. Great Leaders Thank You!!!

And more dynamic special people I car chapter on my special friends but more they are always so genuine Clarissa Wa been in my life for ages and never chan flipped on me one bit), Shakila Quimby Williams-Parker (Ms. Parker), Jessica T Casaia Gaspard, Jackie Wade, Breonna Chakea Davis, Jasmine Latson, Yolanda (Atlanta Mom), April Martin (Atlanta M Lancaster (such a dear friend God sent a divined), Tasia Middleton, Brittany Fraz Jackson, LaTeasa Jackson, Juanita Hosle Lockett. Thank you all so much for bein generous unto me I cannot thank you en

I'm that Girl Only If You Knew

Chapter 1

Can't Get Got

This is my story, and I'm going to give it to you straight "remember", my life is going to prosper and I'm going to succeed by God's grace physically, spiritually, and mentally. I want to tell you all about my college life until present time. I am very private about my life, I always try to remain strong, but go to tell this story. Many may not want to believe, but there is no lie in it. In August of 2011, I entered CAU (Clark Atlanta University) my 1st choice. I was ready to begin I must say. My mom was not prepared for me to take flight lol. Well, l got there and it was on! I moved in my dorm called Bethwick. The first night on campus I could remember it like yesterday. I was with my roommate, and we met up with some other girls to head to a party. I was so ready to enjoy myself—no adults, no parents, no rules, all fun. I met a lot of people. We were vibing to the music, just chilling.

I returned to my dorm around 3 a.m. although I had to go to handle my financial aid and registration for fall 2011 semester. I got up at 7:30 a.m. to head to my school business and it was literally pure you know what... ugh! The lines were incredibly long, and I was so aggravated especially when I found out I had to pay $1,000 upfront for school! I did not have that kind of my money nor my parents because they had bills; I can say it got settled and God spared that.

 As the days began to pass, I moved from Bethwick to CAU girl suites, which weren't traditional dorms due to their very homey feel. There I had three roommates; we were close—well not all—but I was the neutral one. My life was just beginning. I was a Political Science concentration Pre-Law major aspiring to become an attorney. I had the time my life at CAU.

 Every Thursday night I went out to "Thirsty Thursdays" that was the move, my turn-up time. While I was turning up, there was a proper way to do so; I was a classy girl with my girls. I never smoked nor drank and many girls wanted to a part of the crew. During my turning-up time, there was this one guy who approached me with a cup of straight Hennessy. If I had drank that cup, who knows where I would be today. The devil was on my tracks from that day forward.

Soon after, I saw this fine gentleman—6'3, light skin, just how I liked them—but I tried to pay him no mind; I should have continued playing hard to get. However, l must say he got me!!!!! And I mean HE got me. . .

Chapter 2

Miss Thang

It took three months to "cuff me" as they say. I thought to myself, *finally*. Needless to say, I felt that he was the most exceptional man ever if you know what I mean. This situation was a hot mess. First of all, I was a freshman, and he was a junior. Throughout the time of our so-called relationship, I was so young and so dumb. I thought I had it all together, but I just looked like a fool. The link I thought we had was nothing but a daydream/ hope/ game/ booty call/ nothing/ girl get your life. I gave into it so deep to the point I could not see. What I must say I was living in an illusion; I was being used to the utmost: cleaning his dorm, washing his clothes, buying him food, and taking him to work because his car was stolen with counterfeit money. I was a rider, and I wanted to hold him down because I thought we were on the same page—but apparently not. I liked him sooo much because he possessed the physical qualities I wanted in a man, but his intrinsic qualities were not for me.

I thought we had something serious, but the entire time I was being denied and unclaimed. He was messing with so many girls, but he had one special girl whom I was being X'd out for—he only wanted me for hard times. You know what I mean. . . I let it go when I found out after dropping him off at the bus station for Christmas break because he told me he was going home for the break.

Come to find out, I got on twitter and he was posting pictures of him and his special one in an entirely different town from his home. That's why I received no answer or texts back when I checked to see if he had made it home safely. I got played. I just want to advise women out there not to be a fool in love. Love yourself because at the end of the day, self-love is the best love!

I finally opened my eyes and recognized that this was not the Kendra I knew and was raised to become. As my freshman year progressed, I met another guy. I was not into him like he was into me, but honestly, I wasn't feeling anyone. But oh boy! He was a freshman as well a church boy--something

I was familiar with. He had a crew who linked-up with my crew. He was really after me; it was a cute situation. I knew so many females were after him though, and that is why I was not sweating him.

As days and weeks passed, my girls informed me to try it out since he liked me and I could admit I liked him too. Well things got real when his clique started talking to mine in the club just acting like we were the head "you know what" in charge. See the girls and I were a mess—we just knew who we were, where we were headed and what we wanted.

One night, a very cold one, I walked over to his dorm and snuck inside. Mmmmm bad girl college was LITTTTTYYYYYY! In the aftermath of it all, the entire dorm lost their visitation for a month thanks to me. I was caught on camera, but his fellow colleagues were not pressed; they just said "She is pretty." I thought that was quite cute and funny, but I was scared to even walk by that dorm or say Pfeiffer Hall. This guy was very immature as I was used to dealing with older guys. We had chemistry. Things began to get real because later I felt sick one day, very sick.

I was thinking all negative and *I am pregnant*, the worst thoughts due to being a freshman in college and not even married. I always dreamed of being married and financially stable before giving birth to my children. So many thoughts were racing in the head when I hit him up. UH-OHHHHHHHH! He told me, "Let's walk to the store to get a pregnancy test." I was nervous; I could hardly look at him, talk or think about it all. Well, we got to the store and bought the test. I took the test…a straight NEGATIVE!!!!!

God really handled that for real; I dodged a BIG bullet. I never had that happen to me mmm… We talked about it and still were cool, but we began to distance ourselves, especially on my end. It was scary for us, but we still were cool. And I thank God for a new direction; we still are okay till this very day. The end of my first "freshy" semester was near, but it was just the beginning of my journey and the temptation headed for me.

Chapter 3

NOT my CUP of TEA

God had a plan for my life, but I did not want God in it at all—I was all churched out. I was running from him and anything associated with him, yet he continued to chase me. The month of April, 4/20, I was exposed to many things in one night. I tried smoking weed on National Smoke Day or "4/20" for the first time in my life, but I actually did not try to "hit the blunt" as many would say. Someone shot-gunned (blew smoke directly in my mouth) and from that very moment the atmosphere changed—my mind, body, and soul experienced a dramatic shift. The change was sooooo ugly; it was a wake-up call for me, an eye- opener. I remember being in the room as if chains were on me. I felt cold one moment then shaky and hot another. I kept asking people at the smoke party for a bible because I was seeing images that occurred in my childhood and hearing voices. I was flipping through the bible back and forth looking for scriptures asking for forgiveness. I was asking God to save me and cover me under the blood and really acting weird as I can recall.

As I was having this out-of-body experience, I remember seeing strange things—people crawling on the wall and ceiling. The people around me were gossiping about me laughing at my actions. They then started leaving the party. I was lucky God had me in his hands because I soon ran to the store asking for help, but people were just looking at me as if I was crazy. I had on no shoes running for my very life, and I ran across one of the busiest highways in Atlanta, Northside Drive directly by the GA Dome (which is now the Mercedes-Benz Stadium). I was running back to campus, and I remember being on the phone calling pastors in the wee hours of the morning back at home to pray with me.

My mind was all over the place. I called my family asking for their help, and I know they were devastated. My people were 3-4 hours away, so this was a huge scare for them. I saw a police officer who assisted me. He called an ambulance to come get me. No one could understand what happened to me. I should have been dead running onto that highway because that night the traffic was heavy with cars blowing their horns at me. I was not in my right mind at all; I had several flashbacks as a child. And also, I remember seeing a vision of someone knocking on a door saying let me in. I was afraid and still yet distorted as I can recall.

After being in the ambulance and arriving at the hospital, I was placed in a room to detox my body. I remember the doctor telling me that the marijuana was laced with something that was untraceable. I was shocked because I trusted my so-called friends to actually look out for me and not hurt me at this party. That very moment I began to thank God for sparing me because I was in a near-death experience; my heart rate was uncontrollable. I left the hospital thanks to an officer who picked me up and took me back to my dorm at CAU.

Soon when I arrived there, my mother and nana popped up to check on me after driving 3-4 hours to

Atlanta. I started questioning my mom about things I saw the night I had flashback—visions from being an infant, toddler, and present times. We then went to Underground where things enhanced in regards to my out-of-body experience... See, I tried to smoke, and God opened my eyes; what people do not know is the gift of the prophetic is upon my life. I did not know how strong it really was because I thought it was normal seeing things before time and knowing what someone was about to say or even just thinking at the moment. I thought it was still residual effects of that marijuana.

At that nail salon in the Underground, I kept reading people minds literally and asking my mom "Did you hear them?" She kept saying "What are you talking about?" and I felt dumb because I was like *You can clearly hear these people talking.* However, she could not because I was reading them. God enhanced my gift, but I did not know how to control it, so it drove me completely crazy. He was trying to teach me a lesson and show me I needed him and he was not going anywhere.

From smoking that day forward, the devil was after my very own soul. I thought I was crazy because after seeing what I saw that night, many people told me "It's okay, it happens to everyone their first time", and "You just were super high," but seeing that was a wakeup call because I was near death. I was in college not wanting to hear about God nor face him, thinking I am grown now I'm living. I was seeing demons that night which overpowered me. I just thought this is what happens then next time I'll be fine. But for me, there was no next time. After experiencing that, I stayed away from that type of setting. After this issue occurred I just could not sleep because I was scared to go to sleep. I dealt with insomnia for a week in a half. My mom decided I needed to come home after leaving Atlanta that day; I resisted because I had finals coming up for the spring term the end of my freshman year. A family friend drove me home in my car. My mother did not want to hear anything I had to say. She kept saying on the phone while going home "I knew I should have taken you back with me because I do not feel comfortable leaving you in this state."

However, I was instructed by the school to leave campus anyway until I received the proper help and counseling. Upon my return they were going to kick me out. This entire situation affected everything because I had finals and was sent home for two weeks right before them. And also, this mess could go on my record and affect me becoming an attorney. *What if the doctor or counselor who ever tried to diagnose me as schizophrenic?* I could not become an attorney then. I had so many unanswered questions in my head. I kept pitying myself— having to go home made me think that I was going to fail every class in college; but God made a way while I was home. I had the opportunity to complete my assignments while at home. I passed all my classes the end of my freshman year. I was faced with new things that were destined to try and take me out (from being exposed to the guy at Thirsty's trying to give me that Hennessey which I know probably had some kind of drug in it). *Thank God, I did not take it.* Then having the big shebang with the weed (not even hitting the blunt, just simply shotgun) for the very first time. In the midst of it all, I got through even with my first set of college friends returning home leaving CAU. I was still finding me.

Finals ended, classes were over and summer was here. I went to Florida for the summer. I loved Florida. I went to stay with family, my dear cousin whom I love. As I returned home to Jesup, I hung out with my sister and cousin every single day till my sophomore year of college started.

Every day we hung out—we loved to be on ooVoo, take pics, make videos, etc. BTW (by the way) I am the oldest of the two; I even was teaching them how to drive my car. As the days got closer to summer ending, I was so ready to hit the ATL (yes Lord, HOTlanta!). I missed my colleagues and the party life, but this time things were a lot whole lot different. I had an apartment. Yes, Kendra had an apartment y'all !!!! but little did I know mmm. I returned to the ATL and I was exposed to many more things, and I did not ever think the ball would have been in my court at all.

First, I started having roommate problems. The girl's boyfriend had stolen my number out of her phone and started messaging me, sending me disturbing pictures and videos. The entire time I had no idea who it was. Even more interesting, he stated who he was and he was in my apartment alone while I was in my room alone. I just saw him after entering in my apartment from class. My two roommates were gone and I became engulfed with fear. I wanted a way to escape that room. I was stuck due to being alone with a stranger in my own home. I immediately hit up my roommate informing her about the situation because I did not want it to be his word against mine. She rushed home! We wanted him out of our house and the other roommate was not complying. That apartment was the worst decision I made as a semi-adult; it was so much drama. I advise anyone to get your own because you cannot trust everyone nor move in with just anybody.

Secondly, the trend of the city here in Atlanta, I was approached by a man to strip for Magic City. I took the number and thought about it long and really hard. I wanted to but then I didn't align with my morals and standards which were super high. I just could not put myself out there like that although I really wanted the money. I possessed all the looks, the moves, and seduction attributes. And I kept saying what if a family member walked in on me? *Ohhhhh no, that wasn't gonna happen.* My image and character just would not let me at all.

Thirdly, I considered prostitution and escorting. I was thinking *well I can do this…people won't know since it's all private.* Well I got dressed up and went to meet my client. I was scared, very scared, because I was not raised this way and I valued myself and I just saw it as a hustle. My bills were due and I did not want to ask my family for a dime and I was going to do what it took. Well, I entered the room and the man approached me saying "You're very pretty. You look shy." I said, "Sir, I am. I never done this type of stuff and I do not why

I am even here." God was with me. The man told me "You too pretty for this. Are you in school or something?" I informed him I was. He then just gave me the money and told me not to return and get myself together. After that I really thought about it and told myself what you are doing, you are too smart for this. However, I did not let it go all the way. I tried to make a couple rounds, but every time I thought I was gone go I just could not. God would not let me.

So, I finally just stopped the crap and said Kendra, God is trying to spare you from this lifestyle. I was scared to get involved with that mess because I may have ended up on drugs, raped, dead. I was thinking *I can be the next Pretty Woman.* Yeah right, girl no. No one knew about this except my best friend and cousin. I was too embarrassed and ashamed to tell that story because that is not the Kendra they know. I was a modest girl. I was exposed to these things and I stood strong against it. I was a small-town girl in a big city, young, and I did not know I was gone be tempted with these circumstances. By God's grace, mercy, and love he have for me I was in his hand but I still would not reverence him.

Fourthly, I actually had something that changed my path, the path God had in store for me. I got accepted into Georgia State University for spring term 2013. I remember it clear as day. My life was headed in a new direction and my family was excited because Fall 2012, my sophomore year at CAU, I entered Atlanta Metropolitan. My mother thought I was going to be a college drop-out after telling her that I was going to withdraw from CAU. It was God's plan for me to leave CAU to get to where he wanted me to be.

Chapter 4

Everything that Glitters Ain't Gold

Spring 2013 I entered GSU. I continued as a Political Science concentration in Pre-Law major. I was really serious about this lawyer thing; I made it through the largest dilemma moving out of my apartment back to campus but it was best. Arriving at GSU I was nervous, like a freshman all over again. I had some girls who transferred from CAU to GSU which helped me feel a little bit better since we stayed on the same hall. GSU was a new start for me and it really molded me and brought the true good within me out. Although I attended GSU, CAU's motto "find a way or make a way" stuck with me. I struggled badly. I did not have it good with school financially at CAU.

I got to GSU and I didn't have to worry about money for school, but I struggled with academics because I was not focused at all. I was only worried about money, but worrying about that is not going to get no one anywhere but stuck like chuck. My problem was my first job at Perimeter Mall, the clothing store called Body Central. I ended up failing two classes I hit rock-bottom because I completely lost my financial aid. I was working obsessively, not focused on school, but this was the first time I bothered God and wanted him to help me. I felt like I lost everything! *How in the world I was supposed to tell my dang-on parents this mess here?* We were not rich; we had to work for what we wanted, so that meant summer I had to work and pay for my education to bring my GPA from 0.67 to 2.0 in order to receive financial aid. I was going to accomplish it too. I wanted to stay in Atlanta and stay in college, not becomes unhappy, and half-living.

My summer, I returned home having to work and go to school just to get to where I wanted to be. I worked two jobs, drove 30 minutes to work, stood up 5-6 hours, drove back home for 5 minutes from there, headed to job number 2 somedays, then drove an hour to Armstrong University in Savannah, GA from Jesup every day or the off-site in Hinesville. I was a transient student taking 1-2 classes just trying to hang in there having to pay out of pocket.

After summer term I thought I was going to return to GSU. Well God did a U-Turn for me. I thought I was going return, but I did not although I passed my classes. I could not go back because the classes did not qualify for repeat to replace at GSU—you had to take them at GSU not elsewhere. My advisor did not clarify the process for me, so I was extremely mad and upset. I just was like what the heck man I got to finish school and I cannot pay for these classes no more. My GPA was still too low. I was stuck in small ole JESUP, GA. God still had a plan. I had to work to get back on top and honor being able to do so. I worked from retail, fast food paying for just one class all because I did not want to be a statistic and succeed in life. My parents and my grandmother struggled to help me. I remember my mother giving me her entire check going broke just for me to succeed. I was still short. I struggled so much with gas and food; it was very tough, but I didn't give up. Taking two classes Fall

2013, I was only two years away from graduating college. I was so behind from my classmates then. On top of that, I had a long way to go. I went through the motions big time.

Meanwhile, I was home and I met a guy whom I just was talking to. It was nothing super serious, just being young and living. Well, I heard he had HIV/AIDS and I thought *Well I'm no good now. Nobody wants me. What have I gotten myself into?* I sat there praying, begging God to cover me and let there not be one blood cell affected. I was so destroyed. All the plans I had in my life--husband, kids, and family—were being jeopardized all because of my dumb mistakes. My family was so pressed on determining whether I had it, but my mother told me "Get tested. Everything is going to be okay."

Early the next morning, I went to the clinic to get tested. Those minutes seemed as if they were hours. It felt like my life was completely over. My nurse prayed with me and gave me hope. After anxiously awaiting the results from the test, the nurse informed me I was clean. The results were negative! I dodged a bigger bullet and I knew I had to keep my legs sealed. I went back for multiple check-ups, yet nothing showed up. I was completely clean. I moved on, not looking for love because I was broken. My image and character were destroyed from these rumors.

Break ---

Chapter 5

Still At It

So, I stopped writing for a while you guys to focus on school and life. Well, back to my story. I almost forgot to mention way back in 2012 while I was staying in my apartment. There was a guy friend whom I had interest in who I actually thought was capable of building something with me. Well things turned left into a mess! He was someone I really thought I could trust. One day I got in the shower just after arguing, leaving him in my room. The next thing I know, I heard something fall like a big BOOM. I thought my roommate may have dropped something or fell. Well come to find out, after getting out of the shower, it was my brand new 55' flat screen TV that my mother had just bought for me upon moving in the apartment. I was devastated thinking *how a TV just fall off rip like that?* and *now I got to tell my mom this mess.* When I asked him what happened, he said the TV just fell. A TV doesn't just fall. . . COME ON NOW!

I know I just jumped to a flashback, but it got so much worse with him. I got over the TV incident, but Morehouse homecoming was approaching, and I wanted to attend the formal ball. If I did not attend any other event, I wanted to go there. I received a refund from school and went to Lenox Mall to my favorite store, BEBE. I was just looking and saw a little black dress that was very sexy and cheetah high-heels (my favorite! I absolutely love cheetah). I bought a few other things that day. I returned home, placing my debit card on the window sill, and didn't touch it at all while being home.

That night, the guy came over super late after the club and stayed until the next morning. When morning came, I remember going to take a shower. My roommate asked me did I want to go with her to the mall around 12 pm. As I can recall, I got dressed and the guy informed me he was going to leave before I went to the mall. So I walked him out, continued to get dressed and finally left and headed to Lenox Mall. I got to the mall, began to order food and suddenly remembered that I left my card at the house. . . Meanwhile, I was thinking to myself *How did I do that?* Well, the minutes passed and I started getting numerous emails about my bank account. I started scanning the emails thinking *okay when did this occur? I know I'm not getting these emails late. Come on now, I just got my refund. I know exactly what bills I paid and what money I spent.* Well, as I scrolled down, I saw recent transactions within the last 30 minutes for which I was not responsible. I started putting two and two together. I did leave the card on that window sill all day and all night and nobody was in my room but me and him. I thought to myself, *I know this dude ain't just STOLE my money and scammed me like that OHHHH NOOOOOO! I need answers, and I need them quick!*

My mind started racing I was like dang I got played hard and well. To make matters worse, this "fraud" changed the password to my bank account because I saw an email changed password occurred waaaaaayyyy earlier that morning. He had to have done it while I was in the shower because the times on the email were all adding up. Seriously, it does not take a rocket scientist to figure it out. I had my email open on my computer with the password, and username auto-filled—be cautious of that out there; it's a set-up. So, I decided to hit him up immediately. No answer. So, you know I'm 38 hot right now, super ticked off. *First, my TV got cracked all up and now you are playing with my money? Oh no!* Then you're so disrespectful, trying to leave the house before I can even get up good, stole my money and now not ANSWERING THE PHONE ughhh. . . all the hurt all the betrayal. It is one thang to lie, and it's another thang, and I meant THANG to steal from me. There are three things I totally cannot freaking stand it disgusted me: 1) a liar, 2) a thief, and 3) a cheater. That refund from school was the only money I had to pay the remaining bills coming up because working at Body Central was not getting it. The worst part was breaking all this news to my parents and they didn't have any money because they had responsibilities too. Here I was, gullible, thinking I got it all together.

God still was trying to show Ms. Kendra. To make matters worse, I filed a police report on the guy and come to find out the information I had on him was nowhere to be associated with him. He gave me false information about him from the beginning I was so blind to everything. I am going to tell you something—these streets are real and they will swallow you up if you let them. I was really a small-town girl in a big fast city; see I came from a town of everything dirt roads, cotton fields, corn fields, and tobacco fields. I was not warned about the scammers, but baby I had a lot to learn. God still covered me. The bank issued my money back. Thank God! I sure didn't know how in the world I was gone get through this issue here. I was still in my mess and I was not giving God any time nor attention. I am being so real with you all. NADA.

A few months passed by and I met another dude. I just thought *ugh yeah I got this one here*. He had all the physical appearance I want my man to have and he was a Godly man. Oh yes, well it's something about this Godly man. See the Devil knows how to come in and disguise himself. Well the story is a little like this so we can cut to the chase. He told me he was transferred football player from Tennessee University to Georgia State University. He gave me the entire rundown about him and his relationship with God etc. So, you know how us women think—*he's definitely a keeper! He's a man that worships God. We're good then. I can really settle down now.* I'm like *yes, the family is going to love him he ain't going nowhere no sirrrrrreee.* He took me on a little date, stopped by every so often, just very charming and collected. Too good to be true, he was just a scam--all FRAUD!!!! But we will get to that incident a little later. That was a really intense flashback 2012 was tough for me.

Chapter 6

It Got Real

I want to continue back to this HIV thing which occurred in 2013. I posted a status on my Facebook page since so many people including family members thought I was positive. I just wanted to share how I was feeling and clear up my name but my character was crushed.

I opened up a new can of worms in my life, that I surely not ready to handle. This one was a direct assignment to destroy me as a person and all my dreams/goals—I mean a life or death, a real ride or die, a lust/love type of situation. I wanted to be in love and truly loves I was setting myself up for a big downfall.

So, let me get to the tea. Soon after giving the information on what occurred with the HIV situation it was going down in the DM (direct message). I was like *okay it is just, talk I got this.* Why didn't I just stick to that? Just stupid right. I could have just kept resisting but I gave in; it should have been hey and that's that. Things transitioned in my life quickly. We got acquainted things grew but I was not into this guy like any other, I was not looking for a relationship. We just talked. We sat in the car every night for hours having great conversation. I was slowly drawn in the relationship. He told me exactly what he wanted and that's what I wanted. I was like *okay all dudes ain't out to get you lower your standards girl come on.* I thought okay he knew I was serious about a relationship let's really give it a shot. He started doing a lot of things for me that I never was offered by any guy, becoming a better man in many ways, but, more importantly, I was truly happy. Oh, liked that we were making a lot of progress, I did not want to waste my time. This was going to work.

We started officially dating like four months later and things were going great. I was like *we can build something. So, what if he does not have this and that? It is going to get better.* Well something happened on March 26, 2014 that I will never forget. I faced the strangest thing in my life ever. In

March on that day I literally LOST my mind forreal. I remember telling him I wanted to get right with God. I was where I needed to be, I thought. I knew he was the one and I could finally give God a chance because I was satisfied. I was telling him this thinking he wanted to do the same, but I was actually, giving him an ultimatum: God, me, and you or I was going to leave—forcing it on him. I felt like my life was not lined up. I am far from perfect. I was so tired of the same old thing. I wanted to be happy in love and work this thing out. I had so much planned for us and I just wanted God's love and blessings. It all started because I attended a conference in Gatlinburg, TN and God was heavy on my mind. I was caught up but did not want to let him go. I did not want to let anything go—the sex, love, and relationship in general.

Well I told him that I went to sleep and had a dream of someone trying to put spiders and rats on me. I was like *what kind of dream is this is someone trying to hurt me?* Soon after I woke up, I began praying but I let this thing overtake me. I told my mom, but she was getting ready for work. I decided to go see my nana early that morning. She had just had surgery. I had to get to her to tell her about this dream. I remember entering her room, lying on her bed under her, and informing her I wanted to be changed because God was on my mind heavy. I got the bible, just turning the pages asking God to change my heart. She called her Pastor. This thing that was going on inside me was really the makings of me to test my faith and see if I would come to God this time. However, I soon went to the bathroom to take a shower. I remember being in the shower, but after getting out I seemed to start having an out of body experience.

Without knowing, I lost my mind completely. I remember being told I came out the bathroom. I was naked, so my aunts knew something was wrong with me, but what was it? After, being told this and after coming to my senses; I was informed my mother rushed to my nana's to see exactly what was going on with me. She then took me to her pastor to get prayer. It felt just like the first out of body experience but this time it was so ugly. I remember going there. I ran from my mother in a field, steady calling on the blood of Jesus, seeing demons/ spirits, and urinating on myself. I forgot who I was and did not know where I was nor who I was around. I was in a lost world, my mind was gone, I wasn't talking, nor eating, and my entire being shut down. The Pastor informed my mother that someone laid witchcraft on me. WHEN I TELL YOU IT'S REAL, IT IS REAL!!!!! I remember being told they were planning a funeral for me because I was unresponsive and in a daze. I remember my mother and brother pressing through praying for me at ALL night and the bed was shaking. I would not let anyone else talk to me nor touch me but them. I remember sitting up trying to watch T.V.

While watching TV, I began to see pigs, wolves, cats, and etc. so many people looked like animals to me. The sight of it all disturbed me I was destroyed. My mother told me I got a fever and she took me to the emergency room. While there, the doctors informed her they wanted to send me to a mental institution (GA Regional) since there was nothing they could do for me. She fought it because Lord knows going there and having that on my record would have blocked me from pursing any dreams and goals I had for myself. This thing had me bound and so far away from God. I was really in a bad state. My mother was feeding and bathing me just like a newborn baby.

One day in church, a demonic spirit turned my neck completely left and completely stuck. Many thought it would not ever turn back straight but God shamed the enemy breaking this spirit off me. I was running from God. He allowed me to go through this for a reason to see he is God and come to him. After this happened in my life, I tried linking back up with my dude, I decided to live my life I had a rude awakening. In the back of my mind I was just like *someone could not have touched me or did anything to me. I am not bound with witchcraft, NO, NOT ME. I am good.* Months later I received a prophetic word that shocked me on the lines of "...

no man can curse what God has blessed and his grace is sufficient." [2 Corinthians 12:9]

I continued to go to church and stay home but I was not ready. I began to grow very close to a family member, going to their house a lot. I was still worried about my ex because my family made sure we did not have any type of communication after the episode I had. I remember my cousin informing she had a dream about me constantly calling on the blood of Jesus nonstop. It scared me because no one knew I was calling on Jesus except my brother and mother when I was going through. I was scared to really even go around anyone because I knew someone had to lay roots/voodoo on me. I did not know how real black magic really is until it hit my door and it hit it HARD I must say. I contacted my ex because I had so many unanswered questions about my entire experience. I was anxious to know if anyone was trying to hurt me. I knew someone was trying to do something to me after what I faced, but who was it?

God spoke and the word was brought forth and ***"God is not a man that he should lie." [Numbers 23:19]*** and I truly did not want to believe what happened. I just did not know who would do such a thing or could not figure this thing out. It was weird for me because I heard so many people just mention roots/black magic and it is heavy in southern states. In the back of my mind I still had some thoughts about someone putting roots on me. I didn't think I would be exposed to it. I missed my guy and I wanted to make this thing work despite what anyone had to say about any areas in our relationship. Honestly, I was thinking that the stress from school was causing me to have a nervous breakdown. This stronghold was deep in my soul and I just could not shake it. I thought I was covered under the blood of Jesus, but I was not because I was living in sin deeply ask God for repentance and not sincere. Summer was approaching. I got myself together so I could return to Atlanta for school and focus on me. Ret-tooooo-go!(ready)

Chapter 7

Pretty Is As Pretty Does

I packed up my car early to hit the road for summer term in Atlanta at Georgia State. Boy was I ready to leave those backwoods! Just before the semester began, two weeks upon my return to Atlanta, an old guy friend hit me up (the Godly man I mentioned I met in 2012). We engaged in conversation and wanted to spend some time together when I got back in the city. He called me one day explaining to me that he started a new job and needed my help with cashing a check for him. He gave me an entire story about how he needed the check cashed ASAP because he was trying to relocate to another apartment. He even sent a picture of the facility. I wanted to help him. Supposedly his boss wrote out a check and sent it to me. I received the check and cashed it for him and then deposited the money in his account. I was headed for trouble. Less than a week later, the bank called me informing me to come in to talk with them.

When I went to the bank, I found out the check was all fraudulent activity and the check was 2k. I was not trying to get myself in any of this type of mess. He really lied to me. I did not know how in the world I was going to pay this money back. I already was struggling to pay for school out of pocket. I contacted him via phone--no answer. He texted me back way later that week lying about the check. I was crushed!

The devil was right in my face the entire time, but I just could not see that I was being played. I got back to Atlanta for school and I was in my own lane. I did not bother to hit up anyone—no guys, no exes, I was just doing me. Well a couple weeks passed and my exes kept blowing me up wanting to get back together and talk. I was done I thought, but then again, I wanted to try it out again. He told me many things, so I bought into the sweet talk. I set myself aside and tried to try this thing out once more and keep my mind off all negativity.

Meanwhile, being in ATL for the summer and taking 12 credit hours because I was determined to finish college and succeed, I met up with my home girl. The meeting was definitely a divine plan to destroy everything God had planned for me in my life. I was set-up something serious with an opportunity for a better life and doing so I had to engage in sexually relationships. YES, I said it. This friend was setting me up to have a threesome with her guy. I was thinking she and I were trying to play him to just get his money, but the entire time she was in love with him. It was more than what she was telling me. I thought it was just going to be me and him.

Well, she popped up in the room. It was weird. She did not touch me because I was so aggravated. I really felt like they set me up for this, so she can have the luxury life and get what he promised her. I was not with this. I felt so disgusted I removed myself from this situation. I was not so desperate for the lavish life to have sex and entertain females. UH NO MA'AM. I do not like girls and have not ever looked that way plus she was my home girl. And that scheme was an epic fail.

Weeks passed and somehow the guy hit me up for my birthday. I did not know how in the world he got my number because I did not give it to him and my so-called friend made it clear to me to not meet with him unless I was with her. I met him and he gave me many gifts and that was it I thought. Well, she found out of course and things went left. She was upset. WHY? Because they had more than I thought—she was in love with him. I was not even thinking on that level. We were known to just have fun, no sex, get money, and move on. *Were they trying to pimp me, I thought? What is the real deal on this mess?* I did not really know and I did not care to even find out. I cut that off and lived my life. I felt bad and not even for the meet up, simply on that threesome mess. I can honestly say that was a lesson learned. Watch out for those who are your real friends and value your assets.

Summer was ending. I passed all my classes and returned home before fall term I connected back with my guy and I felt complete. I was revived again and wanted what was best for us. I still did not give God any time and he still was not finished. I was ready for senior year. I returned to GSU and the semester went smooth and so did spring. I was passing all my classes, I was faithful to my man, and visited home at least twice a month to see him. Before spring semester ended I found out I could not graduate in summer 2016; I had to go another semester, fall 2016. I was aggravated, but I was almost finished. Climbing the ladder of success is NOT easy!

Chapter 8

Playtime OVER

Finally, summer 2016 was here. I took one class online and I spent time with my man and family. This summer was a big transition in my life and, relationship-wise, things were great. *Yeah, right!* I went to the doctor for my annual exam as I had always done. I definitely knew I was good with my health because I was faithful and so was he. I was not hearing anything about him cheating nor did I suspect anything.

Well two weeks passed by, and I got a letter in the mail informing me that I need to call my OB/GYN office. I called, my heart pounding all the while. I keep reminding myself that the office only calls if the results were positive for something. *Maybe it is minor.* The receptionist picked up the phone and transferred me to the nurse. She stated, "Ms. Fullmore, your results came back and you have not only 1 STD but 2." I immediately became angry, confused, hurt, and numb. I did not know what to say. I had not had sex with anyone and the last time I did I got checked out (I was keen on my health since that AIDS crap). I put all my trust and life in his hands and he took it for granted. *Thank God it was curable, but what if it was not? I have not even had a child yet. What if I cannot have children? What if I'm scarred for life? How I am going to tell my next mate this happened to me if we do not work out?* I had so many mixed emotions, so many. He really could not give me a straight answer on why he did what he did. I kept downing myself. Was I not what he wanted, was I not good enough for him, what was it? I wanted to hurt him in every way possible, but I was stupid and stuck by his side looking foolish and wanting to be loved. My trust began to sway away from him, but I still had some hope; the relationship just became a joke to me. My values and morals disappeared as it seemed. I became lonely and isolated from many. I started losing myself more so now than anything, letting myself go all the way down. I was too focused on making him happy and pleasing him when he did not deserve my love. I really was holding on to this relationship like a thin strand. I wanted to give him another chance thinking it would work.

After facing that, his social media DMs were constantly full, sex began to become the number one priority, the communication vanished, trust was gone, love lingered somewhat, but I was just there pretending things were okay but they were not. Fall semester began and I had to take 21 credit hours and work 3 jobs just to graduate. I did not want to be in undergraduate school any longer. I really did not know how I maintained good grades and lived life.

In this time of my life I was holding down all the weight because my parents were going through a divorce my senior year. I was so destroyed, not understanding it all, and wanted to throw in the towel. And my so-called man could not get himself together even to push and want a better life. He never tried to visit me, simply giving me poor excuses. When you love someone, you will do everything in your might and power for them. I did. When I say I was so far gone in this, I wanted him not really knowing did he really want me. I loved him and cherished him even after his screw ups. In December 2016, I graduated with my BA from GSU. I was confused on everything regarding my life. I had big dreams and goals and my personal life was torn up. I wanted to attend law school immediately after graduating, but the LSAT (Law School Admission Test) was such a challenge for me. So those plans were put on hold. I moved back home and I did not move alone. I let my bf move in and trust me things got real. REALITY hit INSTANTLY. I will never forget it was Christmas Day, my favorite holiday. I was so depressed in bed at a low state in my life. I was over life and anything it had to offer I did not want to get out of bed at all. Many suicidal thoughts were in my head, but I could do such a thing. I was so saddened by the fact I was back home looking for a job in my field, not going to law school, and scrolling on social media seeing all my friends, classmates, and associates living their lives.

Meanwhile, I was home looking for a job with a man who was not providing for me. All the money I got for graduation was spent on everyone and everything but me. I wanted to take a trip out of the country: Jamaica, Dominican Republic, Belize, somewhere. I finally found the strength to get out of bed and write a few scriptures out on flash cards and post them in my room. I was still down with no happiness. A week passed by and I got a job at the bank. I felt a little better about myself, but I just could not satisfy myself with my personal life. I was playing house, not married, half living, and detouring from my goals and dreams. Financial crisis took a deep toll on me and the relationship. I was always in my pockets trying to provide and begging family members to take care of many things. It was a times when I would scrape up $2 or $5 in change just to try to get food or gas. I faced so many circumstances. I put on such a big show for the people on the outside looking in. I started forgetting about what Kendra dreamed to do and began doubting myself. I decided to just forget law school and maybe become a teacher or just get my masters. I wanted to get married and have kids but the reality was how was I going to be able to afford them? I may not even be able to have them, and he was unfaithful before so will he ever be? I could not take care of myself, girl stop. I was not going to church. I had the scriptures in the room but rarely would read them. Soon I started believing there was no God and my thoughts shifted and so did my faith. I was so far from God's presence even after what he brought me through in my life. He held my hand the entire time even when I did not want to live.

At night when I slept, my spirit cried out. I could hear my inner-man weeping and asking for help and direction but yet I still rejected God. I kept asking myself was this the life I wanted to live. Was the relationship really worth it? Was I being pleased with love, care, protection, and financial support? NO! I still endured, until my mother intervened and informed me she was moving back in her home. The entire relationship twisted and I saw all true colors. There was never time for me and things really changed. I was tired because when you love someone I thought you really will go an extra mile for them and beyond. It was like he was depending on me for everything. I started focusing on myself. I took my LSAT again, still yet I did not pass. I cried and moaned but I still did not give in. I soon decided things were not as they should be in my relationship so I wanted out. I felt like it was one of the hardest things I had to face in my life after four years. I was in love with this person which knew my ins and outs; I had to change everything up. I knew I had to focus on me and I was only focusing on other things. I minimized myself and let this relationship drain me and distract me.

On the outside, I looked happy, but deep inside I was so unhappy. I needed to get myself together and leave Jesup so I would not get complacent and stuck. I was bigger than what my hometown had to offer me and I needed to get to a place of destiny. I realized I did not get into law school because I was not ready. I was not focused. It took me years to see I was not focused on anything that is why I faced so many obstacles. These things were to make me stronger and wiser. It's funny to say it because I never thought I would write a book and share these things. But it is to tell the world and bring someone else that may be stuck completely out. Now you can say GAME OVER as I done and live! Nobody can make you choose better for you, BUT you. It begins with your words, ***"Death and life are in the power of the tongue: and they that love it shall eat the fruit thereof." [Proverbs 18:21]***

Chapter 9

No More Sleepin' Beauty but Beauty for Ashes

The GREATEST thing I could ever do was start back attending church. That was the day that revived me to where I needed and was supposed to be. In the midst of it all, attending church was everything. I came back to God and I told God I let everything go. All my life I never fit in nor had several friends, I always tried to place myself with others and things NEVER worked. I also felt out of place I always tried to follow, but God called me to lead. When you obey, you can live your destiny. I felt so much better inside and out. I really felt new because I lost myself as a young woman facing insecurities, emotional distress, and low-esteem *"For I know the plans I have for you," declares the LORD, "plans to prosper you and not to harm you, plans to give you hope and a future." [Jeremiah 29:11]*

God was pulling on me and had my attention. I was so focused on him and my future. I just wanted things in my life to really line up out here in this cold world. It seemed as if love was hard to find in my college life and young adult years, but I couldn't get discouraged and forget that God made me and how he made me. God's love is the best love.

He really protected me and his grace and mercy held me tight. I am not trying to bash anyone in my book. I am not trying to be all deep either. I am being me and informing you all about my life on who/what protects when all else fails. I want to help someone who is in the same place I was once before to value and love his/herself. College students feel so empty sometimes, teenagers, and women, even men. I want to say be obedient to God's commands and your life will unfold tremendously. Self-love is the best love. Worry about you, God, and family and everything else will unfold as well. I know times get hard but DO NOT give up. I worked 3 jobs; went to school full time; almost flunked out; was dumb in love; was used up, chewed up, and spit out; played; and all the things you can possibly name. Yes, I was tired. I was not perfect and still am not, but you have to continue to fight the fight and push. Do not give in. You can make it. I DO NOT CARE who criticizes me on this book. It is my story and I deserve to tell it. I do not hold any bitterness or anger in my heart and I am not ashamed of it. It is my past and I do not live there anymore.

The devil makes us think we are too small, but we are just right because we have to grow bigger to advance. If I did not endure what I did I would not be where I am today and heading—I would still be bound. *"The thief (Devil) cometh not, but for to steal, and to kill, and to destroy: I am come that they might have life, and that they might have it more abundantly." [John 10:10]* I want to say never minimize yourself; never forget who you are or where you come from. Know who you are, your worth, and value. No, I did not have a lavish life. But, trust me; I always carry myself in a respectable way. Do not try to fit in nor aim for something that you are not. YOU have to be uncomfortable in many situations to get you to the place you want to be and need to be. It took me years to learn and I hit my head more than a couple time to get it together. I know the road is not easy but God has you in his hand. Have faith, Remain Humble, and put him first. Be YOU. Do YOU. Love YOU. THIS IS MY STORY!!

Love,

Kendra

Made in the USA
Monee, IL
07 September 2024

64899742R00037